THE ILLUSTRATED MOTORCAR LEGENDS

MERCEDES-BENZ

ROY BACON

PRC

Acknowledgements

The author and publisher wish to acknowledge their debt to all who loaned material and photographs for this book. The bulk of the pictures came from the extensive archives of the National Motor Museum at Beaulieu, and we had kind assistance from Mercedes-Benz itself, and Esplanade Cars, its dealers in the Isle of Wight. Thanks to all who helped.

Text Copyright © 1996 Roy Bacon
Design and layout Copyright © 1996 Promotional Reprint Company Ltd.

Published 1996 by the Promotional Reprint Company Ltd, Kiln House, 210 New Kings Road, London SW6 4NZ.

ISBN 1 85648 362 2

Printed and bound in China

CONTENTS

Karl Benz & Gottlieb Daimler 1885-1925 4

Amalgamation 1926-1939 12

Postwar Revival 1946-1959 24

Into The Sixties 1960-1969 34

The Seventies 1970-1979 48

The Eighties 1980-1989 58

Modern Times 1990-1996 68

List of Models 79

KARL BENZ & GOTTLIEB DAIMLER
1885-1925

MERCEDES-BENZ - an amalgamation of two of the great motor pioneers - one of the most prestigious marques, proud bearer of the three-pointed star, successful in the Grand Prix for decade after decade but also a mass producer which retains its reputation for technical innovation, a high-quality build standard and reliability in use. In essence - builders of some of the best cars in the world.

Both Benz and Daimler took to the road in the 1880s, Karl building his first three-wheeler in 1886, soon followed by two dozen more, all using a single-cylinder, water-cooled 954cc engine. By 1892 Benz was building his Victoria and Vis à Vis models, the latter with the occupants seated face-to-face, and the next year saw the first Benz exported to the USA.

In 1894 the Velo model became the world's first production car, some 1,200 being built over five years, soon joined by the Comfortable which was developed from it, and the Dos à Dos with its back-to-back seating and flat-twin engine. From 1900 Benz cars had front-mounted engines and by 1903 had adopted the format that combined this with rear-wheel drive, metal chassis and two or four-seat body. From then to 1926 the firm built a solid range of sports and touring models.

The start for Karl Benz with three wheels, a single-cylinder and early rack-and-pinion steering.

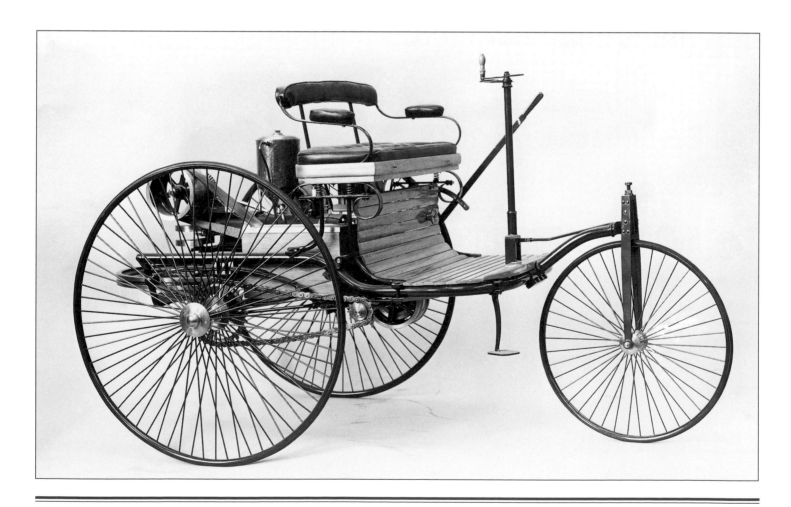

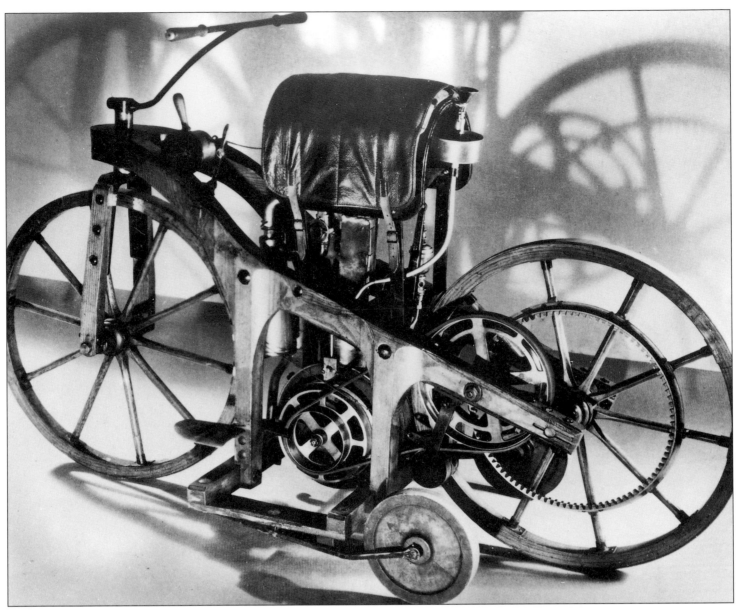

ABOVE: Gottlieb Daimler began with this motorcycle, its wooden frame a means to carry his first engine over the cobbled streets of Stuttgart.

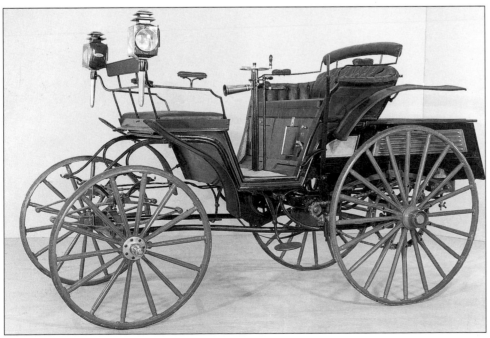

LEFT: A Benz Victoria Vis à Vis where the passengers faced the driver and rode on solid wheels and full elliptic springs.

RIGHT: The world's first production
car, the Benz Velo powered by a
1,050cc single-cylinder engine
producing 2.75hp at 900rpm.

BELOW: Benz Phaeton of 1895 for
eight with Richard Benz at the con-
trols; Karl Benz is in the centre of
the rear seat.

Meanwhile, Gottlieb Daimler built a motorcycle in 1885,and followed this by fitting a 1.5hp, single-cylinder, air-cooled engine into a horse-drawn carriage, it driving the rear wheels via a two-speed transmission. Within a few years he had moved on to water-cooling, four speeds, a V-twin engine, metal chassis and wire wheels. In 1896 he moved the engine to the front of the car - one of the first designers to do so - and in 1901 came the forerunner of the modern car.

The 1901 car was called Mercédès, after the elder daughter of Emil Jellinek, a wealthy Daimler agent who persuaded the firm to design him a lower, lighter and more powerful vehicle. It was among the first to break away from the horse-drawn carriage form and look like a car. The 5.9-litre, four-cylinder engine went at the front, drove a four-speed, gate-change gearbox, and had a honeycomb radiator for its water-cooling system. A channel steel frame carried the mechanics, leaf springs provided the suspension, drum brakes went at the rear, final drive being by chain.

Early Daimler showing the progress being made in the transition from horse-drawn carriage to motor car; also known as the Canstatt-Daimler from the suburb where it was built.

Within a year the Daimler name had been replaced by Mercedes, although the British Daimler ran on to modern times. The new marque soon made its name in sporting events at the highest level while the production models became larger and more powerful with four and six-cylinder engines. By 1908 shaft drive was an alternative to chain and windshields appeared two years later when the firm began to build the Mercedes-Knight cars with sleeve-valve engines. While quiet and powerful, they emitted clouds of oil smoke. Back in 1905 American Mercedes were built by Steinway, of piano fame, in New York but this was not a successful venture.

During the early 1920s Mercedes employed Ferdinand Porsche as chief designer and he took their work on supercharged engines further. Begun in 1921, they had resulted in the 1923 10/40/45, a 2.6-litre, four-cylinder, supercharged model whose 40hp was boosted to 45 when the Roots blower, clutch-driven from the crankshaft, came in as the driver floored the throttle. It forced the air into the carburettor, not the usual arrangement.

A Benz Velo in use in 1898 when the British speed limit was a dizzy 12mph.

LEFT: A true car with engine at the front and rear wheel drive, a 1902 Benz able to seat six in the back.

BELOW: Daimler became Mercedes in 1901, this 60hp model being from 1903 and fitted with a fine four-seater body.

RIGHT: Another 1903 Mercedes 60hp in the form in which these cars were raced when the size of its 9.2-litre engine was nothing exceptional.

BELOW: In 1911 LG Hornstead raced this Little Benz at Brooklands, its 5.7-litre engine having four valves per cylinder.

ABOVE: The Big Benz used by Hornstead at Brooklands in 1913 was a chain-driven, 21-litre monster and set world standing-start records.

BELOW: A six-cylinder 16/50 Benz Sportwagen from the early 1920s, typical of the models listed at that time.

AMALGAMATION
1926-1939

IT was hard for the two firms in the early 1920s so in 1926 they amalgamated as Daimler-Benz, while the cars became the Mercedes-Benz thcy remain to today. Inevitably, at first there were differences between the two rivals now working together, but this soon passed and some fine cars were to emerge in the 1930s.

At first much of the line was prosaic, saloons powered by side-valve, six-cylinder engines and riding on beam axles with mechanical brakes. Names such as Stuttgart, Mannheim and Nürburg were used along with model numbers, and the bulk of the production was of the 8/38hp model 300 of 2 litres. The 12/55 came next, beginning with 3 litres and finishing as the 3.4-litre 14/60 model 350 of 1929. There was also the 15/70hp 400 of 3.9 litres and the massive Model K that had a 6.2-litre engine. The K was based on the similar 630 model and was a big, heavy car; its overhead camshaft engine produced 110bhp, this rising to 160bhp with a supercharger. Fast but hard to stop.

The 1926 Stuttgart 200 was a typically prosaic Mercedes-Benz saloon resulting from the amalgamation.

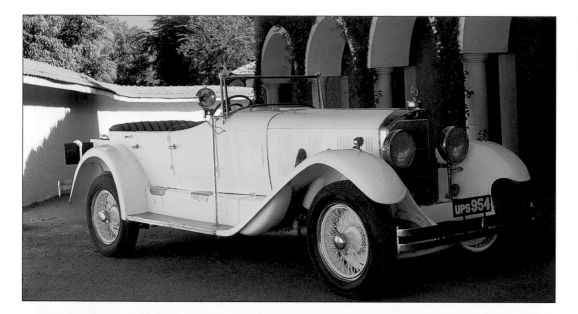

The Type K of the late 1920s had a large overhead-camshaft engine and a shorter wheelbase than usual - K was for Kurz (short).

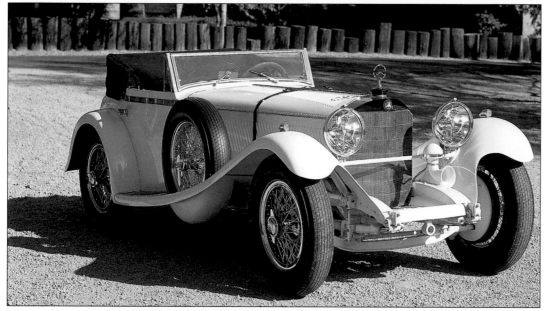

Fabled SSK, Super Sports Kurz, this 1929 example was fitted with a body by Corsica and in due course made a great vintage sports car.

Engine room of a 1929 SSK, the supercharger at the front forcing air into the two carburettors.

The 200 was built from 1932 with a variety of conservative body styles on a chassis with all-round independent suspension, this a 1934 Pullman.

The Nürburg was conventional in body and chassis, built in various styles and produced for a decade from the late-1920s.

The 770 Grosser was the firm's largest model of the 1930s, its production limited and customers distinguished in some way.

For 1927 Ferdinand Porsche introduced the first in a line of classic Mercedes-Benz sports cars - the type S. The 6.8-litre, six-cylinder engine had an overhead camshaft, aluminium cylinder head, twin carburettors and the Roots supercharger brought into play by throttle pressure. It drove a four-speed gearbox, sat in a massive chassis and made a real Mercedes noise while able to top 100mph. Most had an open touring body behind the low-set radiator.

The next year brought the type SS that had a 7-litre engine in the same chassis, a taller radiator, a variety of excellent bodies and 110mph. With it came the SSK, or Super Sport Kurz (short), using a shorter-wheelbase chassis, often fitted with cycle wings, two spare wheels on the back of the fuel tank and a brief body. Producing well over 200bhp when the blower was coupled, it was a big, fast, race winner in the Teutonic style and always expensive.

Finally there came the SSKL, the leicht or light version that had the chassis well drilled to remove weight and give the brakes a better chance of slowing the car. The factory raced them successfully, often fitted with the larger 'Elephant' blower that moved the power up to 265bhp.

Mercedes-Benz went grand prix racing from 1934 and this is the W125 used in 1937 to win many major races. Its 5.6-litre engine delivered over 600bhp.

ABOVE: This 1936 170V retained the all-round independent suspension and was built in various forms including this drophead coupé.

RIGHT: A fine cabriolet 500F from 1936, one of the many models built in the style of that period.

Alongside these charismatic classics, built in small numbers, Mercedes built prosaic, worthy models in far larger quantities. Around this time the firm settled to its practice of indicating the engine capacity in litres by the model number, this was to continue, along with suffix letters, from then on. The 200 Stuttgart was typical, being well made if hardly inspiring, powered by a side-valve six of two litres driving a three-speed gearbox. It stretched to the 2.6-litre 260 with four speeds and a choice of saloon, roadster, tourer and cabriolet bodies.

Larger was the 370 Mannheim with a 3.7-litre engine and built in standard S sport and K kurz (short) forms. The latter had better lines as well as more performance, the first thanks to a pointed radiator in place of the usual dull flat one. Then came the 460 Nürburg with eight cylinders and a conventional chassis in standard or short lengths under a variety of bodies from sports coupé to limousine. In a year or two the original engine was stretched to create the 500N.

The largest Mercedes of the period was the 770 Grosser, built in small numbers, powered by a 7.6-litre overhead-valve, straight-eight engine installed in a conventional chassis carrying an open or limousine body. Most models went to

LEFT: This 1936 200 saloon is another example of the period style on an advanced chassis.

BELOW: A 290 cabriolet from 1936 with the top down, much as the 200 but with a larger engine and just as dependable.

ABOVE: The 500K epitomised the Teutonic sports car of the mid-1930s, less extreme than the SSK, but combining looks with performance.

RIGHT: Frontal aspect of a 1935 500K with spotlight and twin horns to clear its path.

heads of state, or those seeking such status. There was an optional supercharger, the chassis was fully revised for 1938 and from that year the model was only available with the blower.

In 1934 Mercedes-Benz returned to Grand Prix racing, along with Auto-Union, and soon the two German firms dominated the scene, building fabulous cars, far in advance of the opposition over the years until 1939. Inevitably, some of the technical advances appeared on the production models, including the later versions of the 770.

Not all advances had to wait on the race cars: the 170 of 1931 had independent suspension for all four wheels under a conservative body style and was built in quantity in saloon, tourer, roadster and cabriolet forms. Up to 1936 it had a six-cylinder engine but then changed to a four, a backbone frame and a much improved body style; in this form, as the 170V, it would run on postwar. Other models with all-round independent suspension were the 1932 six-cylinder 200 and later 290 types that came in a choice of wheelbase lengths and many body styles up to 1936.

More sporting was the 1933 380K with an overhead-valve, straight-eight, supercharged engine and an improved front-suspension design under a selection of fine bodies. It was not especially fast but led on to the 500K the next year; this

This is a 1936 two-seater roadster version of the 500K showing the great lines that flowed from bonnet to tail.

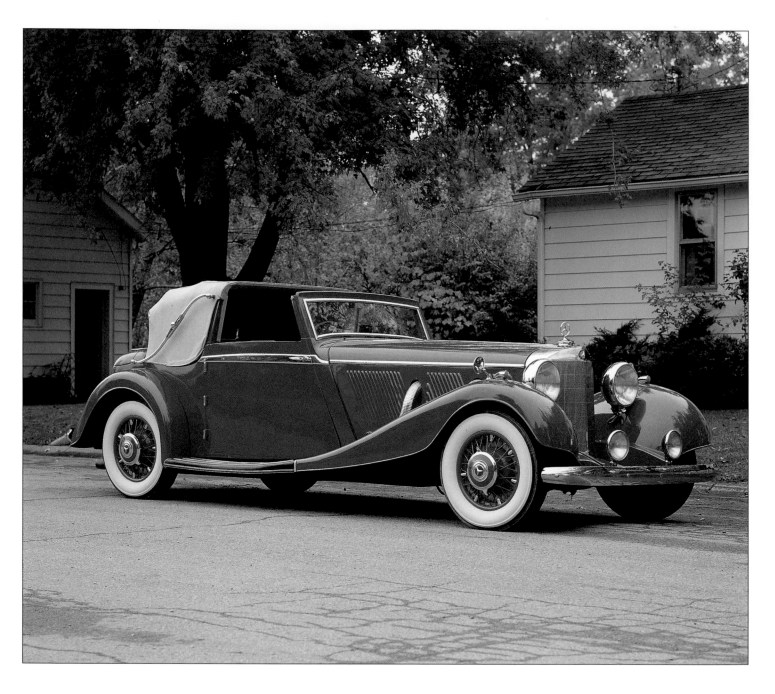

A sedanca drophead 500K, showing another fine body style available in 1936.

had more power, more speed and some of the most attractive saloon and open bodies of the period. Even more expensive was the 540K of 1936 that drank fuel and carried the Teutonic sports car style at its best on up to 1939.

Back in 1934 Mercedes tried a totally different approach with the 130H, which had its engine at the rear in the manner and body style to come with the Volkswagen. It proved to be an unbalanced design due to the engine weight being too far back, and was not a success although built in 150H and then 170H forms to 1939.

In 1936 Mercedes introduced its first production car fitted with a diesel engine, the 260D, based on the 230, also new that year. Both were modest performers, especially the diesel, but had a more modern body style, typical of the late-1930s. The 320 was similar but larger and included a limousine among its body types.

The prewar Mercedes-Benz range was extensive but few cars were built after 1939 when production was turned to military needs. Those which were built were mainly 170V, 230 or 320 models.

ABOVE: Several body types and two chassis designs were used by the 230 models, this one from 1937 shows the improved lines.

LEFT: Rear three-quarter view of a 1936 540K sports model that was powerful and fast, but thirsty.

RIGHT: The cabriolet body on a
540K of 1936: great lines in the
Teutonic style, but an expensive
car to buy and run.

BELOW: With four seats, this
1937 540K has the Cabriolet B
body; the K in the code being for
Kompressor.

LEFT: Rear-engined 130H Mercedes of 1934, innovative but unsuccessful, unlike the similar VW.

BELOW: The basic economy model for most people was the 170V built from 1936 and to continue postwar; this example dates from 1939.

POSTWAR REVIVAL

1946-1959

BASIC transport was the prime need after 1945 and Mercedes-Benz responded with the prewar 170V that was given a number of improvements but retained the side-valve, four-cylinder engine and the same saloon body style. There were also trucks and vans based on the same mechanics, a common practice in those hectic postwar years, and bodies for special needs such as ambulances.

A diesel-powered version, the 170D, was added in 1949 when taxi and station wagon bodies began to be offered by specialist firms, and that year also saw the 170S, the first new postwar model. It had an all-steel body for the saloon and most cabriolets, further refinements, and a slightly larger engine that then became common to the series. Most of the 170 models were dropped after 1953 but a pair of economy versions, using either petrol or diesel power, were built up to 1955.

The 170 ran on postwar up to 1953 and retained its separate head-lamps and side-opening bonnet.

While the 170s plodded on, two new series were introduced for 1951 to move the firm onwards and upwards. The smaller was the 220 that was powered by an overhead-camshaft, six-cylinder engine installed under a body similar to that of the 170 but with the headlights built into the front wings. Saloon, coupé and cabriolet bodies were offered, the saloons sparsely trimmed, and while the style remained prewar, the mechanics were steadily improved.

The second new model for 1951 was the 300 that took Mercedes back into the luxury market, an area that was to grow quickly in the 1950s and one that the company had traditionally always served. The 300 had an overhead-camshaft, six-cylinder engine, twin carburettors, four-speed gearbox and a saloon body, later joined by a cabriolet. It had features such as self-levelling rear suspension and central chassis lubrication among its luxury specification and became popular world wide. It quickly became known as the 'Adenauer' model due to its use by the German Chancellor of the time.

Along with the 300 came the 300S built in small numbers with coupé, cabriolet or roadster bodies on a shortened 300 chassis. The engine was uprated, thanks to a higher compression ratio and a third carburettor, and in 1956 the car became the 300SC with mechanical fuel injection, dry-sump lubrication and a further increase in power from 150 to 175bhp. All were expensive grand tourers and only built in limited numbers, but the 300SC was one of the best cars of its decade.

In 1951 the 220 was added in various body styles but the fixed bonnet sides made servicing hard.

In 1953 the first Mercedes-Benz having unitary construction of chassis and body appeared as the 180. At first it used the side-valve engine from the 170, but this was changed to an overhead-camshaft, four-cylinder type in 1957, in both cases in either petrol or diesel form. A larger unitary model with a six-cylinder, overhead-camshaft engine appeared in 1954 as the 220A. It shared the 180 body, so in that respect moved on from prewar to the 1950s in one leap, built at first only as a saloon and to an austere specification.

The headline Mercedes-Benz news for 1954 was the production version of the 300SL, the model first raced by the factory in 1952 and the Le Mans winner that year. Built only as a coupé at first, this was distinguished by its doors that were hinged in the centre of the roof to rise from the body sides for entry or exit. It was soon known as the 'Gullwing', and this name stuck.

The 300SL had an overhead-camshaft, six-cylinder engine inclined well over to lower the line. It had mechanical fuel injection, dry-sump lubrication, developed 215bhp and drove via a four-speed gearbox to a limited-slip differential. This all went into a tubular chassis that was clothed by a steel body having aluminium doors and access lids; a few were built with aluminium bodies.

The 300SL coupé was built to 1957 during the period when Mercedes-Benz returned to grand prix racing. For 1954 and 1955 they dominated the scene, Juan Fangio taking the title in both seasons. The cars used eight-cylinder engines having desmodromic valve operation and sometimes ran in a fully streamlined form.

A return to the luxury market came in 1951 with the 300, just in time for the German economic miracle of the 1950s.

Expensive but sporting, the 300S had more power, a shorter chassis and a choice of body styles, this one from 1952.

The 300 Cabriolet was based on the saloon and built from 1952 to 1956 in small, exclusive numbers.

Famous 'Gullwing' 300SL model based on the works cars, an advanced and complex car for use on the road.

Such was the effect of the racing successes and the 300SL that Mercedes produced the 190SL in roadster and coupé forms as a lower-priced version, styled on the same lines. While a true sheep in wolf's clothing, it was nevertheless a far more practical car for everyday use and looked sophisticated for a sports car - hence its long production run to 1963 with over 25,000 being built.

To complete the 300SL story there was the Roadster built from 1957, either open or with a detachable hardtop. As with the 190SL, it had conventional doors but under the body it was much as before, simply refined, and while the power went up, so did the weight.

Around 1956 the range moved on. The 180 was joined by the 190 that fitted the overhead-camshaft engine from the start and was offered in petrol and diesel forms. The austere 220A became the 219 and was joined by the 220S that had twin carburettors and was built in saloon, coupé and cabriolet forms, the last two in smaller numbers. Two years later the 220SE with fuel injection was added to the line while the big 300 continued as the luxury model.

RIGHT: By 1956 the sports luxury car was the 300SC with servo brakes and fuel injection, but this is the 300S managing on three carburettors.

BELOW: Success created demand and resulted in this 190SL roadster that offered all the style, if not the Gullwing doors, but much less performance.

Interior of the well equipped 190SL which was able to exceed 100mph, thanks in part to twin carburettors.

The 300SL Roadster had the side vents lacking on the 190SL and the Gullwing mechanics, but not the doors.

ABOVE: The 190 was also available from 1958 as the 190D with a diesel engine; this example dates from 1961 and is pictured in southern Germany.

RIGHT: Based on the 220, this 1958 220S coupé had a later version of the overhead-camshaft, six-cylinder engine.

LEFT: Small numbers of the 220S were built in coupé and, as here, cabriolet form so they were much less common than the saloon.

BELOW: The 220S coupé was rarer than the similar four-door saloon whose line extended the body shape.

INTO THE SIXTIES
1960-1969

AS the new decade began there were changes to the Mercedes range although the faithful 180 and 300 ran on to 1962. The 190SL and 300SL remained as they were, as did the 190, but it was time for a new body style and thus came the series known as 'Fintails' or 'Fin-Backs'.

First to appear, in 1961, were the 220, 220S and 220SE to offer three degrees of tune for the engine taken from the older car, and the usual choice of saloon, coupé or convertible body. The body style was not to everyone's taste, either in Europe or the USA, but it was all new with much improved visibility, space and safety, the last thanks to a crash-testing programme.

Next came the 190 and 190D, built to offer basic reliable transport without much excitement, but for a long time. Top of the line were the 300SE and 300SEL, the latter having a longer wheelbase and extra space for the rear seats to suit limousine use. The engine was the usual six and the four-speed transmission manual or automatic. Self-levelling air suspension and power steering were features of these fine cars.

The old style continued for the 180 and 300 in the 1960s, but this is a 220 coupé demonstrating the 1950s line and its need for revision.

ABOVE: The 190SL continued to look the business in the 1960s, suiting a market that wanted the style without complex mechanics.

LEFT: Roadster 300SL fitted with the factory hardtop to combine style and performance in a desirable package.

RIGHT: Interior of the 300SL, its code on the fascia and moulded into the hardtop, in this case, fitted with a mph speedometer.

New, angular style for the 1960s, shown off by this 1963 220SE convertible that had fuel injection for its engine.

Rear quarter of the 220SE showing
the lines that gave it the 'Fintail' or
'Fin-Back' name.

A true limousine appeared in 1963 as the incredible 600 and introduced a V-8
engine for a production Mercedes. It was built in three forms and the shortest
saloon was a big car. Bigger was the Pullman with its wheelbase extended by
70cm (27.6in) to allow for extra rear seats and, in some cases, three doors on each
side. The third model was the rare Pullman-Landaulet that had a folding rear top.
It was a complex car fitted out to full limousine style with much power assistance
for numerous items.

The 600 engine was a 6.3-litre, overhead-camshaft V-8 with fuel injection producing enough power to push the massive car to 125mph on the autobahn. The
brakes were equally special, transmission automatic and suspension by air. All
told, it was an exceptional car that managed not to be too, too much and was
bought by heads of state, pop stars and those who believed in flaunting them-
selves. There were 2,677 of them and the last was built in 1981.

A new series made its debut in 1963 to replace the older sports models with a
car that was fun to drive at weekends yet still practical for work days. The result
was the 230SL that had a new, fresh style with an angular pagoda-roof form that
was attractive for both the roadster and hardtop coupé bodies. All were two-
seaters, but a third person could squeeze in the back, or an optional child seat
could be fitted. The engine was the well developed overhead-camshaft six with
fuel injection and the transmission had four speeds and either manual or automatic control. The body was steel, but with aluminium doors and covers, and the
whole car exuded quality allied to a 120mph performance.

The original model ran to 1966 when it stretched to become the 250SL and then, in 1968, to the 280SL, its final and most developed form. All were fine cars that did what was expected of them in a good sporting style.

For 1965 the 200 and 200D took over from the 190 models, still with four cylinders but with the extra capacity and twin carburettors to lift the performance while the body stayed the four-door saloon. At the same time the 230 and 230S replaced the 220 models, to be joined by the 250SE coupé and convertible a year later, all with larger editions of the six-cylinder engine. Meanwhile, the 300SE and 300SEL continued as the top of the Fintail line that came to an end early in 1968.

Before then, in 1965, a new body style had been introduced for the 250S and 250SE that increased both interior and boot capacity, kept the six-cylinder engine, but fitted disc brakes all round. A year later the 300SE and long wheelbase 300SEL saloons switched to the new body style while the coupé and convertible ran on as they were.

RIGHT: Top model of the new body style of the early 1960s was this 300SEL, the longer version of the series, stretched for limousine use.

BELOW: Incredible Mercedes-Benz 600 in saloon form, introduced in 1963 and even longer in the Pullman model style with four or even six doors.

ABOVE: Pullman version of the monster 600 built to carry its passengers in great style, comfort and speed; the six doors are most impressive.

BELOW: The regal 600, the rear seats raised, the better to show the occupants to the world at large.

ABOVE: The 230SL was built as a roadster coupé to carry two in comfort or three at a squeeze; it was always a pleasure to drive.

RIGHT: Rear view of the 230SL showing its special roof line, this one from 1966 with right-hand drive.

Around this period the suffix letters of the models began to take on a new meaning. Up to then S usually indicated more sporting by virtue of two or more carburettors, while SE meant fuel injection for the same effect. This changed as what was to become the S-class evolved, this meaning not only a higher than usual performance, but one allied to refined standards of handling and ride for drivers who covered long distances, often with passengers. This designation continues to this day to provide relaxed, speedy and comfortable travel.

There were further changes for 1968 when the new line was joined by the 280S, 280SE, 280SEL and 300SEL, all built in the new style with the six engine. For drivers who sought something a little faster, the factory squeezed the 6.3-litre, V-8 engine into the existing chassis to create the 300SEL 6.3. The result was a 4,000lb saloon car of limited aerodynamics that was still able to reach 60mph in under 7sec and run on to 135mph. Their owners loved them.

The lower end of the range was revised for 1968 with a new body, altered rear suspension and a variety of engines. The 200 and 220 both had four-cylinder, overhead-camshaft engines while the 200D and 220D were the diesel equivalents and the 230 had the six-cylinder engine as did the 250. These saloons were soon joined by two-door, fixed-head coupés that were listed as the 250C and 250CE, the former sometimes fitted with a 2.8-litre engine and the latter with fuel injection.

By 1968 the sporting series had developed into this 280SL, still with the roadster or coupé body and the overhead-camshaft, six-cylinder engine.

ABOVE: The 200 and 200D replaced the 190 models for 1965, had larger engines but kept the body line.

OPPOSITE: This is the 250SE model in its coupé form as built from 1965 to 1967.

RIGHT: The top model of standard length remained the 300SE which adopted the revised rear body style for the late 1960s.

RIGHT: By combining the big V-8 engine from the 600 with the stock body Mercedes-Benz created the 300SEL 6.3 to offer high performance.

OPPOSITE: An angular pagoda-style roof line gave the 230SL a crisp new form, attractive and distinctive to its owners.

BELOW: For the driver seeking a two-door coupé style, the firm offered the 250C and 250CE models from 1969, this one a 1970 build.

ABOVE: A further convertible from the mid-1960s, typical of the Mercedes line at that time, a 220SE.

RIGHT: Front view of the 230S that replaced the older 220 series in 1965 to be the last of the fin-back style

ABOVE: For 1965 there was a new body style, introduced for the 250S and 250SE cars, both with six cylinders and disc brakes.

BELOW: The 280S saloon was built from 1968, also with coupé or cabriolet bodies, and in SE and longer SEL forms.

THE SEVENTIES
1970-1979

THE practice of fitting a larger engine without changing the model code extended in 1970 to add a 2.8-litre 250 and a 3.5-litre 300SEL, while 1971 brought 3.5-litre and 4.5-litre versions of the 280SE and 280SEL plus a 4.5-litre 300SEL. The two larger engines were V-8s and most of these models proved popular and were built in the usual three body styles.

In 1971 a new sporting coupé appeared to launch a SL series to replace the old one. While the roof line remained in its characteristic pagoda style, everything under it was new. The first car was the 350SL that introduced the V-8 engine in a 3.5-litre capacity and a line destined to run for close on two decades. The car was built in roadster and coupé styles, the first with a soft top, the second with a detachable hard-top.

A year later there came the 450SL with a larger engine to lift the performance to 130mph plus, and the 350SLC. This had an extended wheelbase that allowed the addition of two, albeit small, rear seats under the fixed roof. It proved to be an excellent car for work or play.

Fitting a larger engine to an established model became a Mercedes practice in the early 1970s, this car a 300SEL 3.5.

Also new for 1972 were the 280S and 280SE saloons that featured twin over-head camshaft engines and the suspension design taken from the sporting models. Although heavy, the result could run close to 120mph and was well engineered, well built and high on safety. Other new models that year included the 230/4 that used the four-cylinder engine in place of the six, and the 280 and 280E in the same saloon body style. For those who preferred a coupé there were the 280C and 280CE, based on the 250C, and all these 280 models fitted the twin-cam engine.

In 1973 the standard for a luxury car moved up with the arrival of the 450SE and longer 450SEL. To many owners they were simply the best car in the world, regardless of other contenders for that accolade, and combined the V-8 engine, automatic transmission and total sophistication in a 130mph saloon. That year also brought a stretched 450SLC sporting coupé while the lower end of the scale saw the diesel-powered 240D that continued to offer limited performance and minimal charisma but a very long life.

The next year saw the 300D join the diesel line, this having a five-cylinder engine, and the sporting range added the 280SL and 280SLC with the twin-camshaft, six-cylinder engine. In 1975 Mercedes replaced the 300SEL 6.3 with the 450SEL 6.9, thus fitting an even larger V-8 engine to push the car to a comfortable, quiet 140mph allied to a plush ride and fine handling.

Revised for 1971, this is one of the SL series that retained the pagoda roof line, but little else, and was also built as a roadster.

ABOVE: Built from 1972 to 1981 in
350SLC, 450SLC and later 500SLC
forms, this close-coupled coupé
featured a louvered rear side
window.

RIGHT: The 200D fitted with the
1970-style radiator grill, lower and
wider than before, the model
continuing as a basic saloon.

ABOVE: A further study of a 240D that combined the basic excellence of Mercedes-Benz design and technology in an economy package.

LEFT: Economy saloons were built on this body shell from 1968 to 1976 using a choice from four petrol and two diesel engines.

ABOVE: The 200 was the most basic Mercedes-Benz of the mid-1970s with a four-cylinder engine; also listed as the 200D diesel, 200T estate and with larger engines.

RIGHT: From the mid-1970s, Mercedes-Benz saloons kept to a body style that varied little for a decade. The boat lid insignia aided identification.

OPPOSITE: From the front, or in your mirror, it became hard to say if this was a 200D or a 450SEL, until it came past.

RIGHT: The estate body followed the general line of the saloon and used the same range of engines to propel it.

There was a new mid-range style for 1976 offered as the 200 or 230 with the four-cylinder petrol engine, and as the 200D and 240D with the diesel four, or the 300D with five cylinders. With the six-cylinder engine it became the 250, 280 or 280E, the larger size having the twin camshafts.

A year later the coupés joined the saloons in a two-door, five-seat, hardtop form as the 230C, 230CE, 280C and 280CE with the four and twin-cam six engines and a fine body line. For 1978 estate cars appeared in the lists, coded 200T, 230T, 250T, 280TE and 300TD for the diesel. More exciting was the 450SLC 5.0 that fitted a 5-litre, V-8, alloy-block engine of less weight and more power into a car having aluminium body covers to save further weight. It was quick and desirable.

There were other innovations for 1978 including the introduction of ABS brakes, a feature which appeared on more and more models as the years rolled past. The 300SD was the world's first turbocharged diesel car and allied the big saloon to a five-cylinder engine able to haul it along well enough. On the other hand there came the 300CD, a coupé to combine that style with a diesel engine and luxury. At first, its performance was too low to tempt many buyers and, while the style had good lines, the cost and diesel rattle further depressed sales until the engine gained a turbo.

The new series was built on a longer wheelbase in coupé form only as the 350SLC that retained the fine lines of the type.

ABOVE: A new S-class appeared in 1972 as the 280S, 280SE and 350SE, the first two having twin-cam, six-cylinder engines, the third a V-8.

BELOW: From 1973 the 240D was listed, combining the safety and comfort of the fine saloon body with the economy of its diesel engine.

ABOVE: In contrast to the cars having diesel engines, the 450SEL had more capacity, more power and extra length in the rear passenger compartment to be the top 1973 model.

RIGHT: Late in the decade the 450SLC coupé could be fitted with a larger engine and in time turned into the 500SLC before being revised in 1980.

ABOVE: The SL model changed little in overall appearance from 1971 to 1989, but there were many improvements along the way.

LEFT: At first the SL was built in 350 and 450 sizes, later came the 280, 300, 380, 420 and 560, all in the same format.

THE EIGHTIES
1980-1989

THE sports coupé line moved on at the start of the 1980s with the 380SL and 500SL plus longer SLC editions of both, all fitting the V-8 engine. The S-class was now firmly established as the series for successful people who enjoyed their driving but required silence and comfort without losing the sporting feel. For these customers there came the 280SE, 300SE and longer 300SEL as starters while there were the 230CE and 300CE for those who preferred a coupé.

Where a diesel engine was wanted, the estate car gained a turbo to become the 300TDT. The diesel driver was offered a revised S-class 300SD for 1981 while that class added the 380SE and 380SEL saloons and 380SEC and 420SEC coupés that year. The 300D added a turbo to boost its power and performance for 1982.

In 1983 Mercedes-Benz introduced a new entry-level model - the 190. It took the firm back to a smaller car and created a series that would run for a decade in various forms, all using the same basic four-door, saloon body. The engine began as an overhead-camshaft four that stretched to become the 190E 2.3 the next year

The 1980s brought revised versions of the 380SL and 500SL sports coupés, both fitted with V-8 engines and listed in SLC form, this a 500SL.

when the 190D 2.2 with five-cylinder diesel engine joined the series. For 1985 there was the 190E 2.3-16, also listed as the 190 16-V, that had a Cosworth cylinder head with four valves per cylinder and twin overhead camshafts to make a fine performance model without loss of comfort.

Before then the 500SEL and 500SEC saloon and coupé models were added to the series while the 300SL replaced the old 280SL but returned to the single overhead-camshaft, six-cylinder engine. With V-8 power, the 420SL replaced the 380SL while the 250D and 300D, with five and six cylinders respectively, moved that type along and were built with or without a turbo. The 300E replaced an older model and its modest looks belied its good performance, new body, many safety features and improved rear suspension in a package able to outrun many sports models.

The S-class continued development throughout the mid-1980s with the 400, 420 and 500 in SE and SEL forms, joined by the larger 560SEL and 560SEC coupé. The sports coupé line added the 560SL, the smallest diesel grew into the 190D 2.5, the longer 300SDL was added and the 300D Turbo gained a blower to become the world's fastest diesel-powered production car at 127mph. An economy version of the 300E appeared as the 260E using a smaller engine and fewer fittings but making up for this with a lengthy option list. The model was later called the 300E 2.6 and for 1993 it grew to the 300E 2.8.

Rear quarter view of the 500SL roadster with the top down for some open-air motoring.

ABOVE: As an alternative to the saloon line the 230CE gave a fixed-head, two-door coupé.

BELOW: Later 1987 style for both the 230CE and 300CE coupés, both produced for most of the decade.

LEFT: The 240TD model was the result of combining the estate body, able to carry large loads, with the frugal and long-lasting diesel engine.

BELOW: The 190 series became the entry-level model in 1983 and proved most reliable, this being a 190E from the next year.

ABOVE: For performance, this 190E2.3-16 was created using a four-valve Cosworth cylinder head and twin overhead camshafts.

BELOW: Coupé version of the flagship saloon was the 500SEC that used the saloon floorpan for its elegant, two-door body.

Technically interesting and first seen at Frankfurt in 1985 were the 300E 4Matic saloon and 300TE 4Matic estate as both had the firm's four-wheel-drive system. This was fully automatic in operation, engaging the rear, centre and front differentials to suit the traction conditions under each wheel. It was also heavy, expensive and complex but effective where the conditions demanded it. In time, Mercedes developed a simpler system that gave most of the advantages so by 1993 the 4Matic one was dropped.

In 1987 the 200E and 230E were introduced to fill the gap between the 190 and S-class ranges. They were similar to the smaller car but had a longer wheel-base and more room in the rear. Power came from the four-cylinder engine in the two sizes and build quality was to the usual high standard. At the same time the 190D 2.5 added a turbo, the 190E 2.6 appeared using a six-cylinder engine and the 300CE coupé joined the saloon. For the next year the turbo-diesel 300TD estate was replaced by the petrol-powered 300TE and the 190E 2.5-16 offered a little more capacity with the 16 valves.

Another aspect of the 500SEC of the early 1980s when it offered high performance in a fully-fitted car.

RIGHT: Front view of a 500SEC that retained a touch of the old SL roof line and carried its three-pointed star prominently.

OPPOSITE: The sports convertible 300SL that kept the grill style of the past in front of a low bonnet covering much modern technology.

BELOW: A further S-class saloon from the mid-1980s, available in two lengths and engines from 2.8 to 5.0 litres, all being excellent cars.

RIGHT: From the mid-1980s the 300E was listed as a mid-range model, being joined by the 200E and 230E in 1987.

BELOW: Largest of the S-class saloons became the very fully equipped 560SEL of 1986; this is a later model from 1991.

LEFT: This 230TE had a petrol engine and the estate body, while it was also listed with other engines sizes and a choice of diesels.

BELOW: From around the mid-1980s the radiator grill was angled back to improve airflow but lost something of its Teutonic majesty in the process.

MODERN TIMES
1990-1996

THE start of the current decade saw Mercedes-Benz and its range settled in a pattern that had become the norm for the motor industry. The vast costs of designing, tooling and testing called for longer and larger production runs for both the mechanics and the bodies so that manufacturers offered range series that used common components in many ways, listed most engines for most series, and enhanced the result with long option lists.

A new series of SL convertibles appeared in 1990, comprising the 300SL with a twin-cam six engine and the 500SL fitted with a twin-cam V-8. Both were a major step forward and featured an automatic roll bar that raised itself in any potential accident situation, and a fully powered top that latched itself thanks to an array of hydraulics and electrics. Under the stylish body went a five-speed automatic transmission on the 300SL, another first, a suspension system that adjusted itself to suit the conditions and all the refinement, equipment and luxury expected from Mercedes-Benz.

A new SL series appeared for 1990, introducing variable timing to the four-valve heads and a fine new body style.

That year brought a four-valve head and variable-intake valve timing, a feature from the new SL models, for the 300CE. It also saw the 300D 2.5 Turbo in the mid-range body shell, and the 350SD Turbo that used the S-class body. Both performed quietly and well, the larger using a six-cylinder engine. For 1991 they were joined by the longer 350SDL Turbo with the extended wheelbase; this was also the year when Acceleration Skid Control (ASR) took over from the 4Matic system to control wheelspin.

A new S-class saloon series was introduced for 1992 and continued the theme of offering high speed, luxury cruising in the best of environments. Five models were listed, the 300SD with the 3.5-litre diesel engine, the 300SE six, the 400SE

The 300SL convertible had a self-latching power hood and a roll bar that popped up if it appeared to be needed.

ABOVE: Combining Mercedes technology with approved items from an outside source produced the C36 AMG in 1995, a high-speed sporting package.

RIGHT: The new style for the E-class of 1996 as shown by an E230 Classic.

ABOVE: A parked C180 Classic, one of the trim variants listed for the C-class cars.

BELOW: The majority of taxi drivers in Madeira use Mercedes-Benz cars and this is the normal finish, here applied to a C220 diesel.

with 4.2-litre V-8 engine, the 500SEL with longer wheelbase and larger V-8, and the 600SEL. This last not only had the space but its 6-litre engine was a V-12.

Alongside the new S-class cars there were two others, the 400E and 500E. The smaller was a mid-range model on the lines of the 300E but with a 4.2-litre V-8 engine having variable-intake valve timing and 32 valves. The 500E was governed to 155mph, about 10 down on its true potential, and once again Mercedes-Benz had a stock saloon that was the world's best and fastest. Porsche helped with the design of the body shell that was lower and stronger - the result was a great car.

To enhance the performance image of the firm they introduced the Sportline option for the 190E 2.6, 300E and 300CE. This stiffened the suspension, added wider wheels and tyres, and changed the seats, steering ratio and wheel. Engines and transmissions were unaltered but the option improved the handling without impairing comfort.

Largest of the convertible models, the 600SL had a V-12 engine to power its sleek shape to an electronically limited 155mph.

LEFT: Executive E320 for 1994 when the model codes changed to a new form but the engine and body variants continued.

BELOW: Smaller capacity executive E220 that shared the body but had to manage on four cylinders, albeit with 16 valves.

ABOVE: Typical of the S-class, the S280 had the smallest engine and was only built on the standard wheelbase and not to limousine length.

RIGHT: Smallest of the Compact range was this C180 that came in other sizes and a choice of four trims to suit the driver's personality.

More good things came in 1993 with four-valve heads and a 3.2-litre displacement for the 300E and the 300TE estate. The 400SEL joined the S-class line while the 600SL added its V-12 twin-cam engine to the convertible line. The 300CE cabriolet joined the coupé and offered a powered soft top, pop-up rear headrests and other safety measures along with a reinforced chassis. For the driver seeking a coupé there came the 500SEC and 600SEC, much as the saloons with V-8 and V-12 engines, and equally elegant and refined.

For 1994 Mercedes-Benz changed its model codes to three classes: C for Compact, E for executive and S for saloon, plus SL for sporting, with a number to indicate the engine displacement. For some models this simply reversed the existing code to produce E500, SL500 and SL600, but most of the others changed in some way. In place of the 300SL came two cars, the SL280 and SL320, and in the same way the 300SE was replaced by the E280 and E320, and joined by the E200 and E230. With this series came the E250D and E300D with diesel power, E220 and E320 coupés and cabriolets, plus estates with most available engines.

It was much the same for the S-class where the S320, S420 and S500 were listed in saloon and stretched wheelbase forms, the S280 only in the first and the S600 in the second. In coupé form the cars became the S500 and S600, and a S350 Turbodiesel was listed up to 1995.

The C220 model could have either petrol or diesel power, but both engines had four-cylinders and 16 valves.

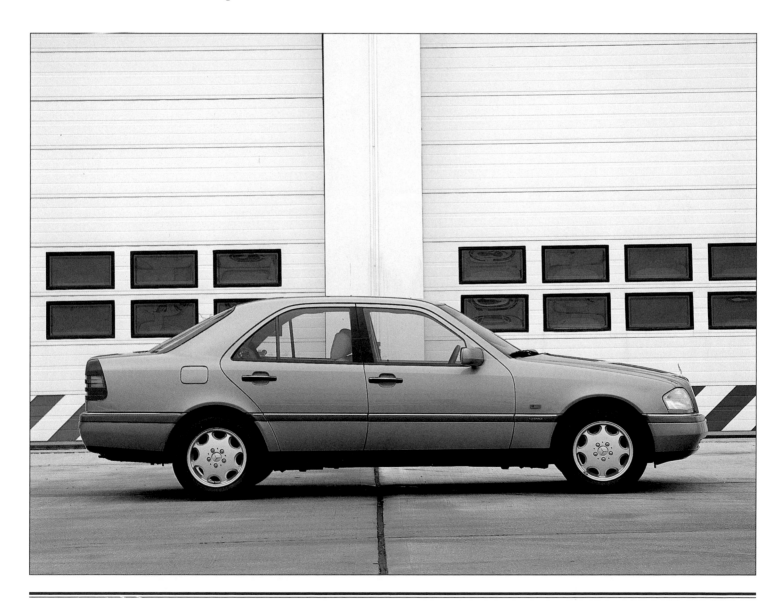

The 190 series was replaced by the C-range compact cars offered with a choice of four petrol or two diesel engines. The first ranged from 1.8 to 2.8 litres and the second came in 2.2- and 2.5-litre forms. Any model was available in one of four style and trim packages; the refined Classic, zestful Esprit, sophisticated Elegance or the racy Sport.

The philosophy of alternative styles and trims was extended to the E-class for 1996 when that series was revised and offered in Classic, Elegance or Avantgarde formats. The C230 Kompressor joined the compact series, this having an engine-driven supercharger rather than a turbo, and later was joined by the SLK 230 Kompressor that put its engine in the sports copé body. They joined the C36 AMG introduced for 1995 that combined items from outside the firm, but fully approved by Mercedes-Benz, with a larger engine, sports wheels, revised body style and other items in a package. This outside supply extended in 1996 to add the E36 AMG in coupé, cabriolet and estate builds.

Thus, Mercedes-Benz drives on to the future behind its three-pointed star, offering some of the very best cars in the world to its customers. To complement these lies a whole fleet of other purpose-designed vehicles for all manner of jobs, but all have their roots in the 1880s when Karl Benz patented his three-wheeler and Gottlieb Daimler went for a drive.

BELOW: The S-class line of S320, S420 and S500 models was available in standard and long wheel-bases, all aimed to provide comfortable and speedy travel.

ABOVE: In this case the model is the E320 Elegance for 1996, combining luxury with quality in all areas.

BELOW: For the 1996 E320 Avantgarde there was lowered suspension, different alloy wheels and a sporting character.

ABOVE: Supercharging returned with the C230 Kompressor model in a refined, mechanically-driven form.

BELOW: A further combination of Mercedes-Benz and an approved outside source introduced this E36 AMG.

MERCEDES-BENZ MODELS

1926-29	400		1954-57	300SL
1926-29	630		1955-58	300SC
1926-29	K		1955-63	190SL
1926-29	8/38		1956-59	190
1926-29	12/55 300		1956-59	219
1927-28	S		1956-65	220S
1928-33	SS		1957-62	180 ohc
1928-32	SSK		1957-64	300SL Roadster
1928	320		1958-65	220SE
1928-29	14/60 350		1958-60	190D
1928-29	460		1959-65	190b
1928-34	260 Stuttgart		1960-65	220
1929-30	350		1961-65	190C
1929-32	SSKL		1961-65	190Dc
1929-33	200 Stuttgart		1961-67	300SE
1929-34	370 Mannheim		1963-66	230SL
1929-33	460 Nürburg		1963-70	300SEL
1930-40	770 Grosser		1963-81	600
1931-39	500 Nürburg		1965-76	200
1931-36	170		1965-76	200D
1931-33	370K		1965-76	230
1931-33	370S		1965-68	230S
1932-36	200		1965-69	250S
1933-34	380K		1965-68	250SE
1934-36	500K		1966-68	250SL
1934-36	290		1968-71	280SL
1934-36	130H		1968-76	280S
1934-35	150H		1968-72	280SE
1935-39	170H		1968-71	280SEL
1935-40	260D		1968-72	300SEL 6.3
1935-42	170V		1968-72	250
1936-39	540K		1968-73	220
1936-43	230		1968-76	220D
1936-41	230L		1969-76	250C
1937-42	320		1969-72	250CE
1938-39	200V		1970-72	280SE 3.5
1946-53	170V		1970-72	300SEL 3.5
1949-53	170D		1970-76	250 (2.8)
1949-53	170S		1971-72	280SEL 3.5
1951-55	220		1971-72	280SE 4.5
1951-62	300		1971-72	280SEL 4.5
1951-55	300S		1971-72	300SEL 4.5
1953-55	170S-V		1971-80	350SL
1953-56	180 sv		1972-80	450SL